Stand in the light

ESPECIALLY FOR YOUTH 2004

Stand in the light

ESPECIALLY FOR YOUTH 2004

DESERET
BOOK

SALT LAKE CITY, UTAH

Contents

1. Stand in the Light   1

2. Child of Light   6

3. His Love   11

4. The Light   17

5. I Was Made   23

6. Here to Be   27

7. Abide with Me; 'Tis Eventide   32

8. See the Light   38

9. Follow the Light   42

10. Calling You   49

11. One Voice   54

12. These Are the Days   59

Stand in the Light

Originally recorded in the key of F♯

Arranged by
TYLER CASTLETON

Words and Music by
TYLER CASTLETON and
STACI PETERS

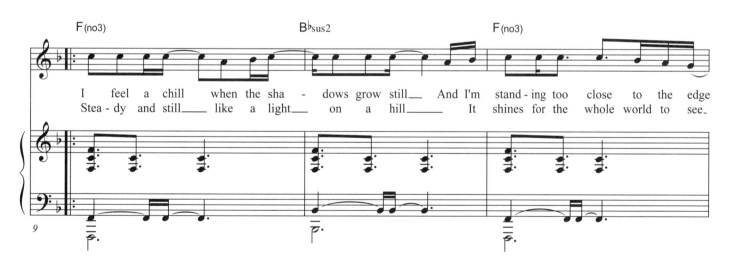

I feel a chill when the sha - dows grow still___ And I'm stand-ing too close to the edge

Stea - dy and still___ like a light___ on a hill_____ It shines for the whole world to see_

2

3

Stand in the light

Stand in the light

I will

Stand in the light_____

Stand in the light_____

5

Child of Light

Arranged by
TYLER CASTLETON

Words and Music by
MINDY GLEDHILL

7

that wants to sing___ And ev-en in___ the deep-est dark-est night___

The torch is raised___ to the sky___ There are hands___ that hold___ it high___

You were born___ to keep___ it burn - ing bright___ You were made___ to fly___

You were meant___ to shine___ Child of___ light___

You were made to fly___ You were meant to shine___

Child of___ light___

10

His Love

Originally recorded in the key of F♯

Arranged by
TYLER CASTLETON

Words and Music by
JAKE RAU

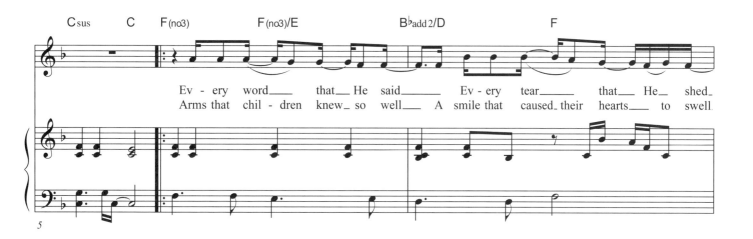

Ev - ery word___ that___ He said_____ Ev - ery tear_____ that___ He shed___
Arms that chil - dren knew_ so well___ A smile that caused_ their hearts___ to swell_

Stays with - in my mind___ and re - minds me of_____ the life___ He led_____
And hands that lift - ed up___ ev - ery time one of_____ his small_ ones fell___

13

for - give_ them_____ for they know not what_ they do"_

Ev - ery pre - cious drop_ of blood_ And ev - ery ounce_ of per - fect_ love_

14

let them   Our o - pen hearts___ would sure - ly feel___

His love

The Light

Arranged by
TYLER CASTLETON

Words and Music by
MICHELLE TUMES

pray That in__ our eyes__ they'll see__ the light__

light_____

I Was Made

Arranged by
TYLER CASTLETON

Words and Music by
MICHAEL WEBB

♩= 74
G
C/G
G
C/G
*He made my
He made my
* Melody originally sung 1 octave lower
G
C/G
G
feet to walk up - on the nar - row road My knees He made to bow and pray
hands to serve the poor and fa - ther - less My arms He made to hold out hope
5
C/G
G
D/F♯
Cadd 2/E
And He made my legs to stand In the light of His love and grace
He made my shoul - ders to bear my bro - thers and sis - ters home
8

*He made my feet to walk up-on the nar-row road___ My knees He made_ to bow___ and pray_____ I was made

Here to Be

Originally recorded in the key of B

Arranged by
TYLER CASTLETON

Words and Music by
TYLER CASTLETON and
STACI PETERS

Pre - cious life___ Ev - 'ry breath is mea - sured___ by the Cap - tain of___ my soul___

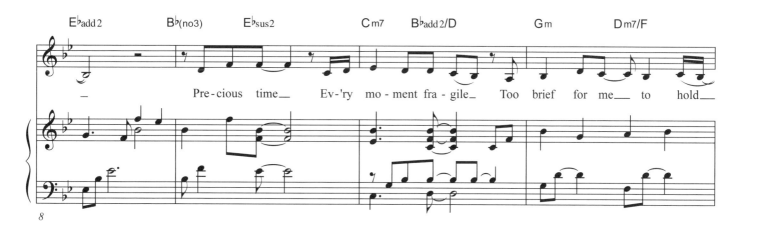

___ Pre - cious time___ Ev - 'ry mo - ment fra - gile___ Too brief for me___ to hold___

Turn the key   Set it free___   Help me see   What You

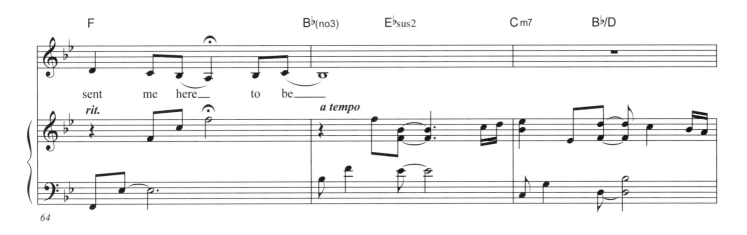

sent   me   here___   to   be___

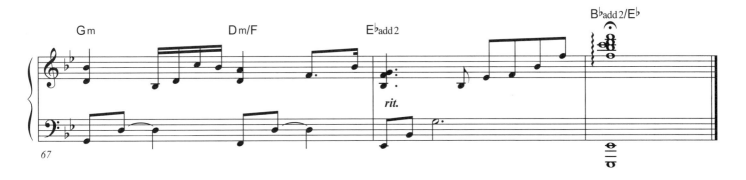

31

Abide with Me, 'Tis Eventide

Arranged by
TYLER CASTLETON

Words and Music by
HARRISON MILLARD and
LOWRIE M. HOFFARD

A - bide with me, 'tis e - ven - tide_____ The day is past and

gone   The shad - ows of the eve - ning fall_____ The

See the Light

Originally recorded in the key of B

Arranged by
TYLER CASTLETON

Words and Music by
JASON BARTON and
SCOTT KRIPPAYNE

*It does-n't mat-ter where you are Or what you're do-ing
All a-round us ev-ery-where are peo-ple hurt-ing

*Originally sung 1 octave lower

You could be some-bo-dy's hope You real-ly don't have to look that far
Op-por-tu-ni-ties to love Make the most of ev-ery day

To see that you can Take the light that lives with-in And
Of ev-ery mo-ment That He gives for us to share

Follow the Light

Arranged by
TYLER CASTLETON

Words and Music by
DON STIRLING, SAM CARDON,
and TYLER CASTLETON

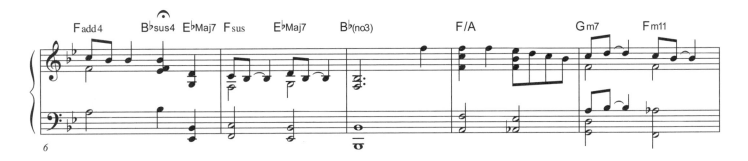

47

48

Calling You

Originally recorded in the key of F

Arranged by
TYLER CASTLETON

Words and Music by
*TYLER CASTLETON and
STACI PETERS*

*You're fad - ing fast___ You're feel - ing help - less and___ a - lone___

6 * Melody to be sung 1 octave lower

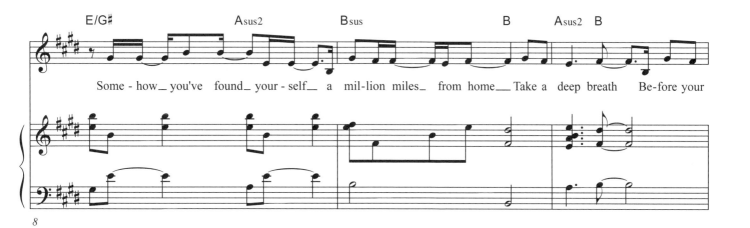

Some - how___ you've found___ your - self___ a mil - lion miles___ from home___ Take a deep breath   Be - fore your

8

One Voice

Arranged by
TYLER CASTLETON

Words and Music by
TYLER CASTLETON and
STACI PETERS

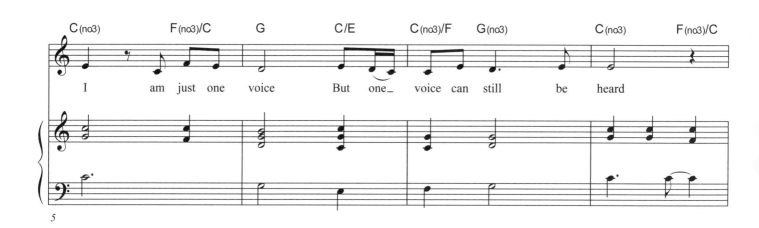

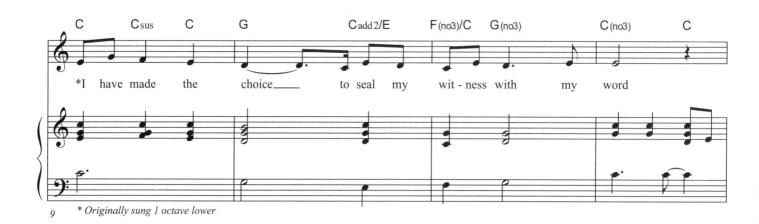

9   ** Originally sung 1 octave lower*

58

These Are the Days

Arranged by
TYLER CASTLETON

Words and Music by
TYLER CASTLETON and
STACI PETERS

Lyrics:

No - ble youth of ev - 'ry na - tion we have heard the call___
We will be the hands of hea - ven mes - sen - gers of God___

Born to lead this gen - er - a - tion___ we are stand - ing tall___ We are
Faith - ful to the gifts He's giv - en___ hold - ing to the rod___ We have

strong___ and we are brave We have___ the cou - rage to o -
hope___ and we have faith We be - lieve___ the world can